Healthcare Power of Attorney & Living Will Kit

by Enodare Publishing

Bibliographic data

- International Standard Book Number (ISBN): 978-1-906144-38-8
- Printed in the United States of America
- First Printing: January 2011

Published by: Enodare Limited
Athlone
Co. Westmeath
Ireland

Printed and distributed by: International Publishers Marketing
22841 Quicksilver Drive
Dulles, VA 20166
United States of America

For more information, e-mail books@enodare.com.

Warning and Disclaimer

IMPORTANT NOTE

This kit is meant as a general guide to preparing your own healthcare power of attorney and living will. While considerable effort has been made to make this kit as complete and accurate as possible, laws and their interpretation are constantly changing. As such, you are advised to update this information with your own research and/or counsel and to consult with your personal legal, financial and medical advisors before acting on any information contained in this kit.

The purpose of this kit is to educate and entertain. It is not meant to provide legal, financial or medical advice or to create any attorney-client or advisory relationship. The authors and publisher shall have neither liability (whether in negligence or otherwise) nor responsibility to any person or entity with respect to any loss or damage caused or alleged to be caused directly or indirectly by the information or forms contained in this kit or the use of that information or those forms.

ABOUT ENODARE

Enodare, the international self-help legal publisher, was founded in 2000 by lawyers from one of the most prestigious international law firms in the World.

Our aim was simple - to provide access to quality legal information and products at an affordable price.

Our Will Writer software was first published in that year and, following its adaptation to cater for the legal systems of over 30 countries worldwide, quickly drew in excess of 40,000 visitors per month to our website. From this humble start, Enodare has quickly grown to become a leading international estate planning and asset protection self-help publisher with legal titles in the United States, Canada, the United Kingdom, Australia and Ireland.

Our publications provide customers with the confidence and knowledge to help them deal with everyday estate planning issues such as the preparation of a last will and testament, a living trust, a power of attorney, administering an estate and much more.

By providing customers with much needed information and forms, we enable them to place themselves in a position where they can protect both themselves and their families through the use of easy to read legal documents and forward planning techniques.

The Future....

We are always seeking to expand and improve the products and services we offer. However, in order to do this, we need to hear from interested authors and to receive feedback from our customers.

If something isn't clear to you in our publications, please let us know and we'll try to make it clearer in the next edition. If you can't find the answer you want and have a suggestion for an addition to our range, we'll happily look at that too.

USING SELF-HELP KITS

Before using a self-help kit, you need to carefully consider the advantages and disadvantages of doing so – particularly where the subject matter is of a legal or tax related nature.

In writing our self-help kits, we try to provide readers with an overview of the laws in a specific area, as well as some sample documents. While this overview is often general in nature, it provides a good starting point for those wishing to carry out a more detailed review of a topic.

However, unlike an attorney advising a client, we cannot cover every conceivable eventuality that might affect our readers. Within the intended scope of this kit, we can only cover the principal areas in a given topic, and even where we cover these areas, we can still only do so to a moderate extent. To do otherwise would result in the writing of a text book which would be capable of use by legal professionals. This is not what we do.

We try to present useful information and documents that can be used by an average reader with little or no legal knowledge. While our sample documents can be used in the vast majority of cases, everybody's personal circumstances are different. As such, they may not be suitable for everyone. You may have personal circumstances which might impact the effectiveness of these documents or even your desire to use them. The reality is that without engaging an attorney to review your personal circumstances, this risk will always exist. It's for this very reason that you need to consider whether the cost of using a do-it-yourself legal document outweighs the risk that there may be something special about your particular circumstances which might not be taken into account by the sample documents attached to this kit (or indeed any other sample documents).

It goes without saying (we hope) that if you are in any doubt as to whether the documents in this kit are suitable for use in your particular circumstances, you should contact a suitably qualified attorney for advice before using them. Remember the decision to use these documents is yours! We are not advising you in any respect.

In using this kit, you should also take into account the fact that this kit has been written with the purpose of providing a general overview of the laws in the United States. As such, it does not attempt to cover all of the various procedural nuances and specific requirements that may apply from state to state – although we do point some of these out along the way. Rather, in our kit, we try to provide forms which give a fair example of the type of forms which are commonly used in most states. Nevertheless, it remains possible that your state may have specific requirements which have not been taken into account in our forms.

Another thing that you should remember is that the law changes – thousands of new laws are brought into force every day and, by the same token, thousands are repealed or amended every day! As such, it is possible that while you are reading this kit, the law might well have been changed. Let's hope it hasn't but the chance does exist! Needless to say, we take regular steps (including e-mail alerts) to update our customers about any changes to the law. We also ensure that our books and kits are reviewed and revised regularly to take account of these changes.

Anyway, assuming that all of the above is acceptable to you, let's move on to exploring the topic at hand.........healthcare powers of attorney and living wills.

TABLE OF CONTENTS

IMPORTANT NOTE 3

ABOUT ENODARE 4

USING SELF-HELP KITS 5

ADVANCE DIRECTIVES – HEALTHCARE POWERS OF ATTORNEY AND LIVING WILLS 9

What Is an Advance Medical Directive? 9
Why Do I Need an Advance Medical Directive? 9
Types of Advance Medical Directives 10
  Living Wills 10
  Healthcare Powers of Attorney 10
Living Wills 11
How Living Wills Work 11
What Is a Terminal Condition? 11
What Is a Persistent Comatose Condition? 12
What Is a Persistent Vegetative Condition? 12
What Life Support Choices Do I Have Within My Living Will? 12
Should I Make a Living Will? 13
State Requirements for Life Sustaining Medical Treatment 15
Witness Requirements 19
Appointing an Agent to Revoke or Enforce Your Living Will 19
Finalizing Your Living Will 20
What to Do With Your Living Will 21
Family Discussions 22
Making Your Wishes Known - Legal Vaults™ Wallet Cards 23
What Is a Power of Attorney? 23
Healthcare Power of Attorney 23
Capacity to Make a Power of Attorney 24
What Does Being "Incapacitated" Mean? 24
Should I Make a Power of Attorney? 25
The Relationship Between Principal and Agent 25
Who Can Be an Agent? 26
Joint or Joint and Independent Agents 26

Alternate Agents ... 27
Scope of an Agent's Powers ... 27
Duties and Responsibilities of an Agent ... 27
Choosing a Healthcare Agent ... 28
Witness to a Power of Attorney ... 29
Commencement of a Power of Attorney ... 29
Revocation of an Advance Directive ... 29
Do I Need Both a Living Will and a Healthcare Power of Attorney? ... 30
Conclusion ... 31

MAKE YOUR OWN HEALTHCARE POWER OF ATTORNEY & LIVING WILL ... 32

APPENDIX 1 - SIGNING INSTRUCTIONS ... 35

Instructions for Completion of the Durable Power of Attorney for Healthcare & Living Will Document ... 36
Instructions for Completion of the Notice of Revocation of a Power of Attorney Document ... 39

APPENDIX 2 - SAMPLE DURABLE POWER OF ATTORNEY FOR HEALTHCARE & LIVING WILL ... 41

Durable Power of Attorney for Healthcare & Living Will ... **43**
Witness Affidavit ... 52
Notary Affidavit ... 54

APPENDIX 3 - NOTICE OF REVOCATION ... 55

Notice of Revocation ... 57
Witness Affidavit ... 57
Notary Affidavit ... 59

ADVANCE DIRECTIVES – HEALTHCARE POWERS OF ATTORNEY AND LIVING WILLS

What Is an Advance Medical Directive?

Have you ever thought about what you would like to happen if an illness or an accident leaves you unconscious or in a coma? Would you want to receive all medical treatments proposed by your doctors? Would you want to forego certain treatments? Would you want to forego certain treatments with a view to allowing for a natural death? Would you want to make these decisions now or have a trusted family member do so at the time and in the full knowledge of the exact circumstances of your injury or illness? Well, now you can make these important decisions by completing an advance medical directive (or an "AMD" as it is also called).

An AMD is a written statement in which you set out the medical care that you wish to receive during any period in which you are unable to make decisions on your own behalf. You can use AMDs to set out your preferences in relation to the receipt and non-receipt of various types of medical treatments and procedures including life sustaining procedures. These preferences will ordinarily be honored by medical personnel if you are admitted to a hospital or healthcare facility; assuming of course they have a copy of your AMD.

Why Do I Need an Advance Medical Directive?

In the absence of having an AMD, state laws will generally allow your close family members to make medical decisions for you during any period in which you are incapacitated and unable to make decisions on your own behalf. While this can of course be beneficial for you, there is always a risk that your family members will make decisions based on what they believe is best for you rather than what you would have actually wanted in the circumstances. More importantly, there is the added risk that the person making these decisions for you might not be someone that you would have entrusted this responsibility to had you the choice. It was in anticipation of these very issues that AMDs were developed. Thankfully, all states now have provisions that allow for the use of AMDs so that people can exercise some control over the medical treatment they receive during periods of incapacity.

Types of Advance Medical Directives

The most common types of AMD currently in use include a durable power of attorney for healthcare and a living will.

States differ widely on the specific types of advance directives they officially recognize. Some also require that you use a specific form for the format and content of your advance directive. If you have specific questions, you should contact an attorney who is familiar with your state's statutes regarding advance directives.

Living Wills

A living will allows you to state whether you want your life prolonged if you are suffering from a terminal illness or in a permanent state of unconsciousness. In brief, a living will indicates whether you want certain treatments withheld or withdrawn if they are only prolonging the dying process or if there is no hope of recovery. As a general rule, living wills only come into effect if you're no longer able to make your own healthcare decisions. For example, if you suffer serious brain damage in an accident or suffer an incapacitating stroke, you may be permanently unconscious and unable to communicate your wishes to your doctor. In this case, a living will lets your physician know your wishes concerning certain life sustaining measures.

Healthcare Powers of Attorney

A healthcare power of attorney allows you to name someone (known as an 'agent') to make healthcare decisions for you if you are unable to do so. A healthcare power of attorney is more flexible than a living will and can cover any healthcare decision, even if you are not terminally ill or permanently unconscious. A healthcare power of attorney can apply in cases of temporary unconsciousness or in case of diseases like Alzheimer's that affect the decision-making process. Like a living will, healthcare powers of attorney allows you to state your wishes about the receipt and non-receipt of certain medical procedures. Also as with living wills, a healthcare power of attorney generally only comes into effect when you are no longer able to make your own healthcare decisions.

We'll discuss each of both living wills and healthcare powers of attorney in turn below.

Living Wills

A living will is a legal document that allows you to express your preferences regarding the receipt or non-receipt of certain life-prolonging medical procedures in the event that you become terminally ill or permanently unconscious and unable to communicate your own wishes. Apart from allowing you to specify your preferences in this respect, it also allows you to designate an agent who has authority to either enforce or revoke the terms of your living will should the agent feel that the circumstances warrant.

How Living Wills Work

In understanding how living wills work in practice, it's important that you realize that living wills only come into effect when:

(i) you are suffering from a terminal condition, a persistent comatose condition or are in a permanent vegetative state;

(ii) there is no real prospect of your recovery; and

(iii) you are unable to make and communicate your own healthcare decisions.

It is only at this point will the person nominated under your living will have any ability to enforce or revoke any of the instructions that you have set out in your living will. However, before this person can lawfully act, the law in the majority of states and indeed the terms of most living wills require that two physicians must first personally examine you and agree that you satisfy the conditions referred to above and that the application of medical procedures would only prolong the dying process. If both doctors agree that this is the case, then the medical procedures may be withdrawn or applied, depending on the choices expressed in your living will.

What Is a Terminal Condition?

A terminal condition is an incurable condition caused by disease, illness or injury with the consequence that there is no reasonable prospect that the patient's condition will improve and the expected result is death. Such diagnoses are often common with progressive diseases such as cancer or advanced heart disease.

Important Note

A terminal condition is referred to in some states as a terminal illness, a terminal injury or an incurable or irreversible illness.

Often, a patient is considered to be terminally ill when the life expectancy is estimated to be six months or less, under the assumption that the disease will run its normal course. In many cases, where people are correctly diagnosed as being terminally ill, they will cease to be able to properly communicate towards the final stages of their illness. It is in these very situations that living wills can be most beneficial.

What Is a Persistent Comatose Condition?

A persistent comatose condition can generally be described as a profound or deep state of unconsciousness where there is no reasonable prospect of regaining consciousness. In other words, while we are in fact alive, we are effectively asleep and unable to respond to life around us. This condition, which is often caused by accidents or traumas, is similar to a coma save that with a coma there is often an expectation that the patient will regain consciousness at some time in the future.

What Is a Persistent Vegetative Condition?

A persistent vegetative state, which sometimes follows a coma, is a condition which results in a person losing all cognitive neurological function and awareness of the environment around them. However, despite this neurological illness, the individual retains non-cognitive functions and a disrupted sleep-wake cycle.

What Life Support Choices Do I Have Within My Living Will?

There are, generally speaking, three different choices you can make in regards to life-sustaining measures:

- Option 1 – You can require doctors do everything in their power to keep you alive.
- Option 2 – You can provide that the only life-sustaining measures you desire to have are artificial tube feeding for nutrition (food) and hydration (water).
- Option 3 - You can have all artificial life-sustaining treatment withheld, including nutrition and hydration.

Of course, you can to a degree mix some of the above options. However, no matter which of these three options you choose, you will generally always be provided with all necessary pain medication and comfort medication. In addition to the provision of treatment for pain and comfort there are a number of different treatments available to help keep you alive including surgery, respiratory support, dialysis, antibiotics, cardiac resuscitation, blood transfusions, tissue and organ donation and receipt of nutrition and hydration.

Should I Make a Living Will?

Whether or not you decide to make a living will is completely up to you. In making that decision, you will need to consider situations that might leave you in a persistent state of unconsciousness or indeed cause your death. Understandably, these are situations you might prefer not to think about. However, with high-tech medicine adding weeks, months and sometimes years to our lives (rather than often adding "life" to our years) we all run the risk of being incapacitated before we die. This leaves some serious questions for you, and indeed everyone, to ponder and to plan for.

Consider what you would want to happen if a serious accident or illness left you in a situation where:-

- you were unable to speak, move, feel or, worse still, you were in constant pain;
- only a respirator and feeding tube were keeping you alive; and
- your quality of life was virtually non-existent and there was no real hope of improvement.

Would you want to stretch your life out on life support or would you rather let nature take its course? Where would you want to draw the line? When should it end?

Unfortunately, far too many people actually find themselves, without warning and without the benefit of asking those questions, in those or similar situations. These people have no control over the medical care they are receiving. These people have no choice but to "live". You can avoid this if you are practical. Consider your alternatives and make a choice.

If this choice is hard for you to contemplate, think of how it will be for your loved ones if you do nothing. If anything should ever happen to you, they will be the ones who will have to bear the emotional trauma of dealing with your permanent incapacity. They will be the ones that will have to visit you in hospital and make the tough decisions for you. They will be the ones who have to consider how to foot the bill for years of hospital care notwithstanding that there might be no possible chance of recovery for you! They may even end up paying these bills themselves!

We don't mean to scare you or to convince you that it's right or wrong to make a living will. We are here to prompt you to think —not to tell you what to think or what you should or should not do or think — just to prompt you into thinking about this very important matter for yourself.

Having the right to deicide what medical treatment you receive, if any, during a terminal illness is what living wills are all about. They allow you to decide these things now, while you can. It is about doing it calmly and without any pressure, and then articulating your wishes in a legal document that will be there to guide your doctors, friends and family if and when you come into the emergency room unable to tell them what you really want. The decision to make a living will is, of course, yours to make!

Important Note

A living will does not allow you to appoint another to make life-sustaining decisions for you; that decision making power can only be granted under a power of attorney. Your agent under a living will typically only has powers to enforce or revoke the decisions you have made in your living will.

State Requirements for Life Sustaining Medical Treatment

Although you may have a living will, certain states have legal restrictions and requirements concerning medical treatment that must be adhered to notwithstanding the terms of your living will. For example, some states require that you receive medical treatment for a certain period of time regardless of your living will. In these states, if you are diagnosed as being in a state of permanent unconsciousness, laws may require that you receive medical treatment for 60 or 90 days before the doctors can make a decision to implement the wishes as set out in your living will. Or if your condition shows zero brain activity, laws may require that you receive medical treatment for a certain number of hours before the terms of your living will can be implemented.

Other legal limitations may also arise. For instance, the provisions in your state may prevent a living will from being implemented if a woman is pregnant, and may declare that the living will is ineffective during the course of the pregnancy.

To be certain of the effectiveness and legality of your living will, and learn what provisos state law may apply, it's best to contact a lawyer in your particular state □ or ask a relevant government agency for information. To give you a flavor of some of the restrictions that apply, we have set out a brief summary of same below.

State	Overview of State Requirements for AMDs
Alabama	Two witnesses required for AMD. An AMD will not be valid if the patient is pregnant.
Alaska	No witnesses required for a living will. Two witnesses are required for a healthcare power of attorney.
Arizona	A witness and a notary are required for both a living will and a healthcare power of attorney.
Arkansas	Two witnesses required for both a living will and a healthcare power of attorney. Neither will be valid if the patient is pregnant.
California	Two witnesses required for both an AMD and a healthcare power of attorney. A healthcare power of attorney can also be witnessed by a notary.
Colorado	Two witnesses required for an AMD. A healthcare power of attorney does not require any witnesses.
Connecticut	Two witnesses required for both an AMD and a healthcare power of attorney. The signatures must be notarized. Neither will be valid if the patient is pregnant.

Delaware	Two witnesses required for both a living will and a healthcare power of attorney.
District of Columbia	Two witnesses required for both a living will and a healthcare power of attorney.
Florida	Two witnesses required for both a living will and a healthcare power of attorney.
Georgia	Two witnesses required for both a living will and a healthcare power of attorney. A living will is not valid if the patient is pregnant.
Hawaii	Two witnesses required for both a living will and a healthcare power of attorney. The healthcare power of attorney must be notarized. A living will is not valid if the patient is pregnant.
Idaho	Two witnesses required for both a living will and a healthcare power of attorney. A notary can also witness a healthcare power of attorney. A living will is not valid if the patient is pregnant.
Illinois	Two witnesses required for a living will. A living will is not valid if the patient is pregnant. One witness required for a healthcare power of attorney.
Indiana	Two witnesses required for a living will. A living will is not valid if the patient is pregnant. A notary is required for a healthcare power of attorney.
Iowa	Two witnesses and a notary required for both a living will and a healthcare power of attorney. A living will is not valid if the patient is pregnant.
Kansas	Two witnesses or a notary are required for a living will.
Kentucky	Two witnesses or a notary required for a living will. A living will is not valid if the patient is pregnant.
Louisiana	Two witnesses required for both a living will and a healthcare power of attorney.
Maine	Two witnesses required for both a living will and a healthcare power of attorney.
Maryland	Two witnesses required for both a living will and a healthcare power of attorney.
Massachusetts	No provision for a living will. Two witnesses required for a healthcare power of attorney.
Michigan	No provision for a living will. Two witnesses required for a healthcare power of attorney.

Minnesota	Two witnesses and a notary required for both a living will and a healthcare power of attorney. A living will is not valid if the patient is pregnant.
Mississippi	Two witnesses required for an advanced healthcare directive (includes both a living will and a healthcare power of attorney in the one document).
Missouri	Two witnesses required for both a living will and a healthcare power of attorney. A notary can also witness a healthcare power of attorney. A living will is not valid if the patient is pregnant.
Montana	Two witnesses required for a living will.
Nebraska	Two witnesses and a notary required to witness a living will.
Nevada	Two witnesses required for both a living will and a healthcare power of attorney. A notary can also witness a healthcare power of attorney.
New Hampshire	Two witnesses or a notary required to witness both a living will and a healthcare power of attorney.
New Jersey	Two witnesses or a notary or a lawyer is required to witness both living wills and healthcare powers of attorney.
New Mexico	No witnesses required for either a living will or a healthcare power of attorney.
New York	Two witnesses required for both a living will and a healthcare power of attorney.
North Carolina	Two witnesses required for both a living will and a healthcare power of attorney. A living will is not valid if the patient is pregnant.
North Dakota	Two witnesses required for both a living will and a healthcare power of attorney. A living will is not valid if the patient is pregnant.
Ohio	Two witnesses or a notary required for both a living will and a healthcare power of attorney. A living will is generally not valid if the patient is pregnant.
Oklahoma	Two witnesses required for both a living will and a healthcare power of attorney. A living will is not valid if the patient is pregnant.
Oregon	Two witnesses required for both a living will and a healthcare power of attorney.

Pennsylvania	Two witnesses required for a living will (includes a healthcare power of attorney in the same document). A living will is not valid if the patient is pregnant.
Rhode Island	Two witnesses or a notary required for both a living will and a healthcare power of attorney. A living will is generally not valid if the patient is pregnant.
South Carolina	Two witnesses or a notary required for both a living will and a healthcare power of attorney. A living will also requires a notary to act as a witness.
South Dakota	Two witnesses required for both a living will and a healthcare power of attorney. A healthcare power of attorney can also be witnessed by a notary. A living will is generally not valid if the patient is pregnant.
Tennessee	Two witnesses required for both a living will and a healthcare power of attorney. A healthcare power of attorney can also be witnessed by a notary.
Texas	Two witnesses required for both a living will and a healthcare power of attorney. A living will is generally not valid if the patient is pregnant.
Utah	Two witnesses required for a living will. A living will is generally not valid if the patient is pregnant. A notary is required for a healthcare power of attorney.
Vermont	Two witnesses required for both a living will and a healthcare power of attorney.
Virginia	An advance medical directive requires two witnesses.
Washington	Two witnesses required for a living will. A living will is generally not valid if the patient is pregnant. No witnesses are required for a healthcare power of attorney.
West Virginia	Two witnesses and a notary required for both a living will and a healthcare power of attorney.
Wisconsin	Two witnesses and a notary required for both a living will and a healthcare power of attorney. A living will is not valid if the patient is pregnant.
Wyoming	Two witnesses are required for both a living will and a healthcare power of attorney. A notary is also required for a healthcare power of attorney. A living will is not valid if the patient is pregnant.

Witness Requirements

In order to ensure that a living will is the voluntary act of the person making it, and that this person has not been unduly influenced by their medical condition or by other persons, certain states have limitations on when a living will can be made and who can serve as witnesses.

In several states, you cannot make a living will while you are in the hospital or in a nursing home. It must be made before you go to the hospital (or at least, after you have been discharged, and before you're readmitted with your 'final illness'). In other instances specific conditions will apply before you can make a living will in hospitals. For example, under Georgia law, if you wish to make a living will while you are a patient in a hospital or resident in a nursing home, you will need to have an additional person to witness you signing your living will form. In the case of a hospital, this third witness must be the chief of the hospital staff or a physician not participating in your care. In the case of a nursing home, it must be the nursing home's medical director or a staff physician not participating in your care.

In most cases, you will need two witnesses to witness the signing of your living will. However, you should be aware that a number of states prohibit certain people from acting as a witness to the signing of a living will. In fact, some of the state forms expressly specify who cannot act as a witness. You should be sure to check the laws of your state to determine who can and cannot act as a witness to your living will. In general, however, the following people are precluded from acting as witnesses in most states: your spouse, children, grandchildren, parents, grandparents, siblings, or any lineal ancestors or descendants. Also included are spouses of any of these people. Other persons who should not be witnesses of course would include a person who is named in your last will or who would benefit from your estate (if you died intestate), someone who is a beneficiary of a life insurance policy on your life and finally a person who is directly responsible for your medical care (including employees, agents and patients of any hospital or nursing home that you might be in). The rationale here is that each of those people may potentially gain upon your death and may make decisions based on self-motivation.

You should also avoid using minors or anyone named as an agent in your healthcare power of attorney.

Appointing an Agent to Revoke or Enforce Your Living Will

As already mentioned, some states allow you to name an agent who may either revoke or enforce your living will. It is generally considered that when you name an agent, you are giving that person the power and authority to go to court on your behalf and ask a judge to either revoke or enforce the terms of your living will. However, in some cases, depending on the content of your living will, the agent does not need to go to court, but can merely instruct the medical care providers to either disregard or to enforce your wishes as set out in the living will. Alternatively, the agent may only be able to temporally suspend the operation of your living will so that it is not used at a specific time, but may be used later.

Important Note

Even if you don't appoint an agent under your living will, healthcare facilities and physicians are still obliged to follow the provisions set out in your living will.

Appointing a person to enforce or revoke your healthcare decisions can be useful because it allows for advocacy on your behalf which could help get over difficulties in interpreting your living will. It's also worth remembering that if a physician refuses to respect the terms of your living will you have the right to be transferred to another physician or hospital that will honor the document. An agent can be very useful in ensuring that this happens.

Finalizing Your Living Will

Once you have decided to make a living will, you should check the specific laws that may apply in your state. Many states have specific forms and, in a few states, required language that should be included in your living will. We have included a form in the back of this kit which complies with the requirements of the vast majority of state laws. In practice, as most states recognize living wills made in other states, most medical practitioners will recognize living wills of varying kinds provided that that they are properly executed. Nevertheless, it would be prudent for you to review the laws of your state to ensure that the sample living will complies with those laws (which of course change quite frequently). Once you have done this, there are a few final steps you should take to ensure that your wishes will be respected when the time comes:

- you should discuss the terms of your advance directive with your doctor before you sign it. Make sure you are both comfortable with what it says. He or she may suggest something you hadn't thought of that you might decide to include;

- comply with your state's signature and witness requirements. As mentioned above, states have various requirements about who can be a witness, how many witnesses are needed, and if the directive must be notarized; and
- provide copies of the signed directive to (1) your doctor and hospital; (2) your agent if one is named; (3) family members; (4) your lawyer and (5) other significant people in your life.

Out-Of-State Directives

People often wonder whether advance directives made in one state will be honored in other states. The good news is that the laws of many states provide for the recognition of living wills made in other states. However, there are some states where the law is simply not clear on the issue. While there is a degree of ambiguity in these states, the practical reality is that most healthcare providers will try to abide by your wishes irrespective of whether you use an out-of-state form or not.

In situations where you spend much of your time between a few different states, it might be useful to make a living will in each state just to cover off the possibility that a healthcare provider refuses to recognize an out-of-state living will. It might even be practical to have different healthcare agents in each such state but this is something that you will have to consider carefully.

What to Do With Your Living Will

After you have properly signed your living will, and had it witnessed and notarized, you need to take it to your doctor. (NB: this is not to get the doctor's advice. You've already done that before you finalized your living will.)

Ask your doctor to make a copy of the original living will and to put the copy in your medical records so that he/she will have it for future use. Keep the original living will in a safe place. If you go to the hospital, take the original living will with you.

What Do I Do With My Living Will After Completing It?

The original should be kept in a safe place with all your other important papers and legal documents. Copies should be given to your doctor, agent and other close family members to ensure that it's available when needed. It's also a very good idea to carry a small card in your wallet or purse that states that you have a living will and provides contact details for a person or organization that can provide it to medical personnel when required

Ask the hospital personnel to make a copy and put the copy in your medical records. Put the original living will back in a safe place. This should not be somewhere which is hard to access, like a safe deposit box, just in case somebody you hadn't thought of needs to see it and you aren't able to communicate at the time.

Family Discussions

In reality, if you become incapacitated, it will be up to your family to decide whether or not they wish to support the end-of-life decisions that you have made in your living will or whether they will try and fight it with a view to keeping you alive or allowing you to die naturally. It is for this very reason that we recommend that you discuss your personal choices with close family members. At the very least, it will afford you an opportunity to bring them around to your way of thinking. Alternatively, it will open the door for a discussion that may provide you with useful feedback or may even present you with alternatives that you had not considered.

In having this discussion, you should explain to your family members the decisions you have made and why you have made them. Remember, it's important that you also try and get them to accept the person that you have nominated as your agent under your living will. Otherwise, in addition to the emotional trauma, your family could find themselves amidst a grave conflict should you become incapacitated. It follows that it is also very important that you discuss your wishes with your agent and ensure that he or she is fully aware of what you want to happen should you ever become incapacitated. If you get both your family and agent in line with your thinking on the subject, matters should hopefully run smoothly as between them when the time requires.

Making Your Wishes Known - Legal Vaults™ Wallet Cards

When you have made your advance medical directive, it is a good idea to carry a card in your wallet or purse confirming that you have done so. This way, if you are admitted to a medical facility and unable to communicate, healthcare providers will be alerted to the fact that you have set out your requirements in relation to end-of-life treatments can get a copy of your AMD and will be legally bound to honor your wishes. By including on your card the contact names and numbers of key family members, details of your doctor and details of the location of your advance directives if you have any, your healthcare providers will be able to determine your healthcare wishes when most needed.

Important Note

For more information on obtaining wallet cards and storing your advance directives electronically so that physicians and medical personnel can easily access them in a time of emergency we recommend visiting the Legal Vaults™ website at www.legalvaults.com.

What Is a Power of Attorney?

A power of attorney is a legal document by which you can appoint and authorize another person (usually a trusted friend, family member, colleague or adviser) to act on your behalf and to legally bind you in that respect.

The person giving the power of attorney is referred to as the 'donor', 'grantor' or 'principal', while the recipient is called the 'agent', 'attorney-in-fact' or just plain 'attorney' (which doesn't mean they have to be a legal practitioner!).

Healthcare Power of Attorney

One of the most common forms of power of attorney in use today is the healthcare power of attorney (also known as a medical power of attorney).

A healthcare power of attorney allows you to authorize an agent to make healthcare decisions on your behalf should you be incapacitated and unable to do so. The authorization conferred on your agent can cover any form of healthcare decision and applies even where you are not terminally ill or permanently unconscious. It also applies in cases of temporary unconsciousness (if you were in an accident, for instance) or in cases of mental diseases like Alzheimer's disease which affects the decision-making process. The important point to remember is that, unlike certain other forms of power of attorney, it does not automatically terminate if you become incapacitated – in other words, it's durable! In fact, in many cases, the agent's authority under the power of attorney only comes into effect when the principal becomes incapacitated!

With a healthcare power of attorney, you can specify guidelines and directions regarding the medical treatment that you want to receive during any period in which you are unable to make healthcare decisions on your own behalf. Save in the most extreme cases, your agent will be obliged to follow these instructions. You can also give your agent full freedom to make healthcare decisions on your behalf during any period in which you are incapacitated.

Capacity to Make a Power of Attorney

Generally, anyone who has reached the age of majority in their state and who has sufficient mental capacity can make a power of attorney. However, the precise requirements for making a power of attorney differ from state to state. As such, if you are in any doubt as to whether you can make a power of attorney, you should seek the advice of a practicing attorney in your state.

What Does Being "Incapacitated" Mean?

You will be deemed to be 'incapable' or 'incapacitated' if you are unable to understand and process information that is relevant to making an informed decision and if you are also unable to evaluate the likely consequences of making that decision.

The decision as to who determines whether you are incapacitated or not is generally set out in your healthcare power of attorney. Generally, it will state that two doctors or attending physicians must agree that you are incapable before you are actually deemed incapacitated and your power of attorney comes into effect.

While it may be somewhat obvious, it's worth pointing out that you must be mentally capable of granting a power of attorney at the time when the document was signed. This generally means that you must, if required, show that you are aware of the nature and extent of your assets and personal circumstances and that you understand your obligations in relation to your dependants and the nature of the power being granted to the agent under the power of attorney.

If you are found to be incapable or incapacitated in a time where you believe you are not, you have the right to request a capacity review hearing for the purpose of affirming or quashing that determination. You will have the right to be represented by counsel at that hearing. Agents appointed under a power of attorney have a general duty to explain this right to you and cannot try to prevent you from contacting a lawyer or asking for a review hearing. This said, it should be remembered that unless the agent is a professional accustomed to acting under a power of attorney, the likelihood is that the agent will not be aware of his obligation in this regard.

Should I Make a Power of Attorney?

If you would like to specify the specific forms of medical treatment that you would like to receive and/or have withheld during any period in which you are unable to make those decisions yourself, then it is a good idea to have a power of attorney. Similarly, if you want to appoint someone you trust to make these decisions for you, a healthcare power of attorney can be very useful. In most cases, if you don't make a healthcare power of attorney, your attending medical team will usually take instructions from your close family members.

The Relationship Between Principal and Agent

One of the principal features underlying the relationship between a principal and an agent is the requirement that the agent acts with the utmost good faith on behalf of the principal. It is a relationship built on trust in which the agent is obliged to act with loyalty on behalf of the principal and in accordance with instructions received from the principal. The agent can neither intentionally ignore these instructions nor negligently act in the performance of them. In return for this loyalty, a principal instills confidence and trust in the agent thereby creating a fiduciary relationship of trust and confidence between the parties. It is this relationship of trust and confidence that underlies every specific action taken, or left untaken, by the agent.

Unfortunately, human nature being what it is, the principles of trust upon which the fiduciary relationship is built are often honored more on paper than in observance. The reality is that people sometimes succumb to the pressure of other affairs, to a lack of thought about and appreciation of their obligations, and of course to temptation. This risk of breach is the primary risk associated with agency relationships particularly because of the agent's ability to bind the principal.

Who Can Be an Agent?

While there is no need for an agent to be a professional person, he or she must be an adult capable of making decisions and carrying out specific tasks on your behalf. What's more, if the specific power of attorney you intend to create is one for healthcare, it may be advisable to weigh the agent's capacity for compassion as more valuable in this instance than their talents as a financial analyst or businessman.

The agent cannot be an un-discharged bankrupt and should not be the owner, operator or employee of a nursing home or extended care facility in which you are resident. Neither can the agent be a witness to your signature on the power of attorney.

Joint or Joint and Independent Agents

Sometimes a principal will want to appoint one or more agents to act on his/her behalf. Where the principal makes such a decision, he or she needs to decide whether the agents will be 'joint' agents or 'joint and independent' agents.

Joint agents must act together. As such, they must unanimously agree on a course of action before that action can lawfully proceed. Furthermore, in taking any action, joint agents must take the same action at the same time. For instance, if one of the agents is missing or unwilling to engage in a specific action, the remaining agents are powerless to act. This type of arrangement adds a degree of protection to the principal as it removes the possibility of any of the agents acting carelessly or selfishly. 'Joint and independent' agents, on the other hand, can act either together or individually. As such, while both or all agents may be acting on behalf of the same principal and in relation to the same matter, they will not be obligated to consult with each other before taking an action which can bind the principal.

In the ordinary course of things, it is recommended that you avoid appointing joint agents. Rather, if more than one is to be appointed, it is preferable to appoint agents as alternates to the original agent.

Alternate Agents

While it is not necessary to do so, it is always a very good idea to appoint an alternate agent (also known as a substitute agent). The authority conferred on an alternate agent will only come into effect where the primary agent is unable or unwilling to act on behalf of the principal. In such circumstances, the alternate agent will acquire full power to act (unless expressly restricted) under the power of attorney.

In many cases, medical facilities will require proof that the original agent is unable or unwilling to act as agent under a healthcare power of attorney before accepting instructions from the alternate agent. In such cases, it's often useful for an alternate agent to request a signed confirmation from the principal revoking the authority of the original agent or, if unavailable, from the original agent confirming in writing his or her refusal or inability to act as agent.

Scope of an Agent's Powers

Your agent will have as many or as few powers as you specify in your power of attorney. Generally, a healthcare power of attorney will give an agent authority to consent, to refuse to consent, or to withdraw consent to any care, treatment, service, or procedure to maintain, diagnose, or treat a physical or mental condition on behalf of the principal. The scope of this power is generally subject to any limitations that the principal includes in his power of attorney document.

However, it is important to remember that within the scope of the authority you confer on your agent he or she can do anything that you can legally do.

Duties and Responsibilities of an Agent

Generally speaking, your agent has the duty to act in your best interest, to act towards you with the utmost good faith and to avoid situations where there is a conflict of interest.

Choosing a Healthcare Agent

The person you choose to be your healthcare agent should be a trusted individual who is also knowledgeable and comfortable discussing healthcare issues. Because this person may need to argue your case with doctors or family members, or even go to court, an assertive yet diplomatic individual may be the best individual to represent your interests. Your representative should be well aware of the choices you have made in your advance directives and should support those instructions.

For most, the person chosen to act as an agent is a spouse, partner or close family relative. However, while you of course trust these people you will need to consider whether they have the resolve to make the tough decisions that you have asked them to make when the time comes. If you are in any doubt, you may wish to chose an alternative agent or appoint a second agent who independently has full authority to carry out your instructions. However, we would not ordinarily recommend the appointment of joint agents as it can lead to arguments and conflicts between them which result in delays in important medical decisions being made.

In choosing an agent, you should consider the person's age, emotional ability, how well they know you, their views on your wishes and the right to life generally, their religious beliefs, whether they have any financial or other interest in your survival or death and the availability of that person generally to act as your agent.

In certain states, a spouse can lose the right to act as an agent for his or her spouse if the couple are legally separated or divorced unless you provide otherwise in your healthcare power of attorney.

Similar to the position with living wills above, your agent or healthcare proxy should not be someone attending to your healthcare as there is a danger of a conflict of interest arising in such circumstances as it is in the healthcare provider's financial interest to keep treating you rather than curing you!

Important Note

As a practical matter, it's useful to appoint the same person as your agent under both your living will and healthcare power of attorney – of course, the choice is up to you in this respect!

Witness to a Power of Attorney

You should have at least two people witness your signing of the power of attorney. To satisfy various state requirements, it is advisable that you not use any of the following people as your witnesses:

- your spouse;
- your partner;
- your child;
- your agent or alternate agent;
- the spouse of your agent or alternate agent; or
- employees of a medical facility in which you are a patient.

Your witnesses must be of legal age in your state. They must also have legal capacity and be of sound mind.

Commencement of a Power of Attorney

A power of attorney will start on a date specified in the document or, in some states, upon the occurrence of a specified event such as incapacity. If there is no specified date or event, a power of attorney starts immediately upon notification to the agent, following its execution by the principal and appropriate witnessing.

A healthcare power of attorney can be drafted to start at either the time of its signing or upon the incapacity of the principal.

Revocation of an Advance Directive

Provided you are not incapacitated, you can revoke an advance directive at any time by sending a 'notice of revocation' to your agent and/or to anyone who might rely on the directive. This is a written legal notice signed by or on behalf of a person who made the directive stating that he or she is terminating the powers conferred on the agent under the advance directive and cancelling all directions given in that document.

There are a number of reasons, practical and personal, why you might want to revoke an advance directive. These may be that:

- the advance directive is no longer necessary as you are now able to act on your own behalf;
- you no longer trust the agent who is acting on your behalf;
- you have found a more suitable person to act as your agent;
- it is no longer practical to have your agent acting on your behalf;
- you have changed your mind in relation to the directions and choices set out in your advance directive; or
- the purpose behind originally granting the power of attorney has been fulfilled and you no longer need an agent to act on your behalf.

The revocation of an advance direction is not effective against the agent or any third party who may rely on it until such time as notice of the revocation has been received by that party. As such, it is common practice to have a written notice evidencing the revocation rather than simply trying to revoke the authority orally. This written document can, in turn, be sent (by recorded delivery, if necessary) to all third parties (especially medical personnel) who may rely on the advance directive to put them on notice that your agent's authority has been revoked and the medical decisions and choices expressed in your advance directive no longer apply or have effect. You should send the notice of revocation to any medical practitioner who holds a copy of your advance directive.

A sample form of notice of revocation is contained at the back of this kit.

Do I Need Both a Living Will and a Healthcare Power of Attorney?

Most estate planners agree that the best approach in dealing with healthcare issues is to have both a living will and a healthcare power of attorney. As already pointed out, using a living will in isolation is problematic as it only relates to end-of-life decisions. As such, in order to cover all other medical decisions, it is generally advised to make a healthcare power of attorney to supplement it. It's even better when you can combine both into one document as it lessens the likelihood of any conflict arising where there are two separate documents. In fact, many states allow you to combine the two documents.

Conclusion

You now have two important ways to prepare for the possibility that you may sometime be unable to decide for yourself what medical treatment to accept or refuse. You should consider the use of a living will and a healthcare power of attorney carefully as they form an integral part of estate planning.

Make Your Own Healthcare Power of Attorney & Living Will!

Now that you understand what a healthcare power of attorney & living will is, how it operates in practice and the importance of having one, it's time for you to consider making your own. At the back of this kit, we have included a sample healthcare power of attorney & living will form. A brief description of this form is set out below:

- Has wide scope and covers your healthcare and medical affairs. You are free to choose the scope of your agent's authority and to direct your agent regarding your preferred medical treatment.
- Also includes details of your wishes regarding end-of-life medical treatment.
- Agent's authority only commences following a medical determination that you have become incapacitated.
- Agent's authority terminates (i) when you revoke the agent's authority, or (ii) on your death. You could also amend the document to state that the authority of your agent will end at a specific time or on the occurrence of a specific event.
- Not terminated by incapacity and operates during any period in which you are incapacitated.

We have also included a Notice of Revocation of a Power of Attorney at the back of this kit for your convenience.

Before using any of the forms in this kit, you should carefully review them in order to ensure that they meet your requirements and are suitable having regard to your particular circumstances. If you are in any doubt as to the suitability of the documents for your use or the scope of the documents, you should consult an attorney before using these documents. If you decide to use any of the above mentioned documents, be sure to read the document in full and follow the signing instructions carefully. Remember, these documents are provided on an 'as-is' basis and the decision to use them is yours.

IMPORTANT NOTICE

This document will give the person you name as your agent the power to make medical decisions on your behalf. This power is subject to any limitations that you expressly include in your document. After you have signed this document, you will still have the right and authority to make medical decisions for yourself if you are mentally competent to do so.

APPENDIX 1

SIGNING INSTRUCTIONS

Downloadable Forms

Blank copies of this form are available to download from our website.

Web: http://www.enodare.com/downloadarea/

Unlock Code: YUK20150

enodare

Instructions for Completion of the Durable Power of Attorney for Healthcare & Living Will Document

1. Carefully read all the instructions below.

2. Print out the document which you intend using and complete it neatly using a pen or carefully edit the text version of the form (that is available to you to download) on your computer.

3. On the cover page of the document, insert the date of execution of the power of attorney as well as your name, as principal, in the spaces provided.

4. The first paragraph of the document identifies the person making the document. In this paragraph, you will need to enter (i) your name and address and (ii) the state in which you reside.

5. In clause 1.1, enter the name, address, home telephone number and work telephone number of your primary agent in the spaces provided.

6. In clause 1.2, enter the name, address, home telephone number and work telephone number of your alternate agent in the spaces provided.

7. In clause 1.3, enter the name, address, home telephone number and work telephone number of your second alternate agent in the spaces provided.

8. In clause 2.1, you are asked to initial one of the two choices available in each of sub-clauses (i) to (iv). Simply insert your initials in the space provided opposite each of the choices you wish to select. Read each of the choices carefully before initialing your preferences.

9. In clause 2.1(v), you can insert any further instructions you wish. If you insert any instructions, you will need to initial the space opposite where you have included your instructions.

10. In clause 6.1, you can specify your end-of-life wishes. The sections are divided into three parts namely (i) terminal conditions, (ii) permanent unconsciousness, and (iii) maximum treatment. You can either choose to receive the maximum treatment possible in all respects under part (iii) or you can choose to receive or not to receive treatment subject to

a few exceptions under parts (i) and (ii). You can choose to complete part (iii) alone or parts (i) and (ii) together. You must choose one or the other of these two options (assuming you wish to complete this part of the document).

Once you have decided what options you wish to select, sign your initials beside your chosen options. If you have chosen options (i) and (ii), then you will need to specify whether you want treatment applied or withheld in each case. If you wish to have treatment applied, you should place your initials beside the word "shall". If you wish to have treatment withheld, you should place your initials beside the words "shall not". Once you have done this, you should place your initials beside any specific treatments that you want to receive. If you do not want to receive a specific treatment, do not place your initials beside that treatment.

11. In clause 7, please select your preference for the administration of treatment for the relief of pain. Please initial one choice only.

12. In clause 8, if you are female, please indicate whether your preferences in relation to end-of-life treatment should continue to apply if you are pregnant. Please initial once choice only.

13. In clause 9.1, please indicate whether you would like to make a donation of your organs following your death. You have three choices – give no organs, give any organs needed or specify your gift in your own words. Please initial one choice only. If you chose to specify your gift in your own words, make sure to complete the section as concisely as possible.

14. If you have decided to gift any organs under clause 9.1, you will also need to complete clause 9.2. In clause 9.2, you can specify the purposes for which you are donating your organs. Please sign your initials beside the purposes for which you are donating your organs. You can choose as many preferences as you wish.

15. In clause 10, you will need to insert details of your primary physician. Your primary physician will have primary responsibility for determining whether you are suffering from a terminal condition or are in a state of permanent unconsciousness. In this clause, you should specify the name, address and telephone number of your primary physician in the spaces provided. You should also specify the name,

address and telephone number of your alternate physician in the spaces provided.

16. Arrange to meet with a notary. Once you meet the notary, you should proceed to step 17 – in the notary's presence.

17. In the execution block, immediately after clause 11, enter the date, month, year, place and state of execution. Then sign your name on the signature line above the words "Signature of Principal" in the presence of the notary and two witnesses.

    Your witnesses should not be a person who is:

    - your agent or attorney-in-fact;
    - the notary acknowledging your signature;
    - a relation by blood, marriage, or adoption to you or your agent; or a spouse of any such person;
    - financially responsible for your medical care;
    - entitled to any portion of your estate following your death;
    - a beneficiary under an insurance policy on your life;
    - entitled to make a claim against your estate (such as creditors); or
    - your attending physician, nor an employee of such a physician.

18. You should have the two witnesses who witnessed your execution of the power of attorney complete the "Witness Affidavit" section of the document.

19. You should then have a notary complete the "Notary Affidavit" section of the document.

Instructions for Completion of the Notice of Revocation of a Power of Attorney Document

1. Carefully read all the instructions below.

2. Print out the document which you intend using and complete it neatly using a pen or carefully edit the text version of the form (that is available to you to download) on your computer.

3. On the cover page of the document, insert the date of execution of the notice of revocation as well as your name, as principal, in the spaces provided.

4. The first paragraph of the document identifies the parties to the original power of attorney and its date. In this paragraph, you will need to enter (i) your name and address, (ii) the date of the power of attorney and (iii) the name of your agent.

5. Arrange to meet with a notary. Once you meet the notary, you should proceed to step 6 – in the notary's presence.

6. In the execution block, enter the date, month, year, and place of execution. Then sign your name on the signature line above the words "The Principal" in the presence of the notary and two witnesses.

   Your witnesses should not be a person who is:

   - your agent or attorney-in-fact;
   - the notary acknowledging your signature;
   - a relation by blood, marriage, or adoption to you or your agent; or a spouse of any such person;
   - financially responsible for your medical care;
   - entitled to any portion of your estate following your death;
   - a beneficiary under an insurance policy on your life;
   - entitled to make claim against your estate (such as creditors); or

- your attending physician, nor an employee of such a physician.

7. You should have the two witnesses who witnessed your execution of the notice of revocation complete the "Witness Affidavit" section of the document.

8. You should then have a notary complete the "Notary Affidavit" section of the document.

APPENDIX 2

SAMPLE DURABLE POWER OF ATTORNEY FOR HEALTHCARE & LIVING WILL

Downloadable Forms

Blank copies of this form are available to download from our website.

Web: http://www.enodare.com/downloadarea/

Unlock Code: YUK20150

enodare

DATED THIS ____ DAY OF ____________, 20___.

____

DURABLE POWER OF ATTORNEY FOR HEALTHCARE & LIVING WILL

of

____

(Principal)

____

NOTICE: THIS IS AN IMPORTANT LEGAL DOCUMENT. IT GIVES THE PERSON YOU DESIGNATE AS YOUR AGENT THE POWER TO MAKE HEALTHCARE DECISIONS FOR YOU. SPECIFICALLY, IT GIVES AUTHORITY TO YOUR AGENT TO CONSENT, TO REFUSE TO CONSENT, OR TO WITHDRAW CONSENT TO ANY CARE, TREATMENT, SERVICE, OR PROCEDURE TO MAINTAIN, DIAGNOSE, OR TREAT A PHYSICAL OR MENTAL CONDITION. THIS POWER IS SUBJECT TO ANY STATEMENT OF YOUR DESIRES AND ANY LIMITATIONS THAT YOU INCLUDE IN THIS DOCUMENT. IF THERE IS ANYTHING IN THIS DOCUMENT THAT YOU DO NOT UNDERSTAND, YOU SHOULD ASK A LAWYER TO EXPLAIN IT TO YOU.

www.enodare.com

DURABLE POWER OF ATTORNEY FOR HEALTHCARE & LIVING WILL

I, ________________________ of ________________________________, being of sound and disposing mind and having attained the age of majority in the state of ________________________ make this Durable Power of Attorney for Healthcare & Living Will.

PART 1 - DURABLE POWER OF ATTORNEY FOR HEALTHCARE DECISIONS

1. DESIGNATION OF AGENT

1.1 I appoint the following individual as my primary agent:

Name: ____

Address: ____

____

____

____

Home Telephone: ____

Work Telephone: ____

1.2 If I revoke my primary agent's authority or if my primary agent is not willing, able, or reasonably available to make a healthcare decision for me, then I appoint the following individual as my alternate agent to make such decisions on my behalf:

Name: ____________________

Address: ____________________

____

____

____

Home Telephone: ____________________

Work Telephone: ____________________

1.3 If I revoke the authority of my primary agent and my first named alternate agent or if neither is willing, able, or reasonably available to make a healthcare decision for me, then I appoint the following individual as my alternate agent to make such decisions on my behalf:

Name: ____________________

Address: ____________________

____

____

____

Home Telephone: ____________________

Work Telephone: ____________________

2. AGENT'S AUTHORITY

2.1 I hereby authorize and direct my agent to follow my individual instructions and my other wishes to the extent known to the agent in making all healthcare decisions for me. If these are not known to my agent, then my agent is authorized to make these decisions in accordance with my best interests, including decisions to provide, withhold, or withdraw artificial hydration and nutrition and other forms of healthcare to keep me alive, except as I otherwise state herein:

Note: In each of (i) to (iv) below, initial one choice only!

(i) _____ I grant my agent power to withhold or withdraw life-prolonging procedures in accordance with my instructions herein.

_____ I do not grant my agent power to withhold or withdraw life-prolonging procedures.

(ii) _____ I grant my agent power to withhold or withdraw artificial hydration and nutrition in accordance with my instructions herein.

_____ I do not grant my agent power to withhold or withdraw artificial hydration and nutrition.

(iii) _____ I grant my agent the power of control over the disposal of my remains and organ donation decisions subject to my instructions herein.

_____ I do not grant my agent any power of control over the disposal of my remains and organ donation decisions.

(iv) _____ I grant my agent the power to consent to or refuse an autopsy being carried out on my remains.

_____ I do not grant my agent the power to consent to or to refuse an autopsy being carried out on my remains.

(v) ____

____

____

____

3. WHEN AGENT'S AUTHORITY BECOMES EFFECTIVE

3.1 My agent's authority shall become effective when my primary physician, or in the case of emergency an attending physician, determines that I am unable to make my own healthcare decisions.

4. AGENT'S OBLIGATION

4.1 My agent shall make healthcare decisions for me in accordance with the instructions set out herein and my other wishes to the extent known to my agent. To the extent my wishes are unknown; my agent shall make healthcare decisions for me in accordance with what my agent determines to be in my best interest. In determining my best interest, my agent shall consider my personal values to the extent known to my agent.

4.2 Accordingly, save as otherwise may be provided herein, my agent is authorized as follows:

(a) to consent, refuse, or withdraw consent to any and all types of medical care, treatment, surgical procedures, diagnostic procedures, medication, and the use of mechanical or other procedures that affect any bodily function, including, but not limited to, artificial respiration, nutritional support and hydration, and cardiopulmonary resuscitation;

(b) to authorize, or refuse to authorize, any medication or procedure intended to relieve pain, even though such use may lead to physical damage, addiction, or hasten the moment of, but not intentionally cause, my death;

(c) to authorize my admission to or discharge, even against medical advice, from any hospital, nursing care facility, or similar facility or service;

(d) to take any other action necessary to making, documenting, and assuring implementation of decisions concerning my healthcare, including, but not limited to, granting any waiver or release from liability required by any hospital, physician, nursing care provider, or other healthcare provider; signing any documents relating to refusals of treatment or the leaving of a facility against medical advice, and pursuing any legal action in my name, and at the expense of my estate to force compliance with my wishes as determined by my agent, or to seek actual or punitive damages for the failure to comply; and

(e) to request, review, and receive any information, verbal or written, regarding my physical or mental health, including, but not limited to, medical and hospital records and to consent to the disclosure of this information.

5. NOMINATION OF GUARDIAN

5.1 If a court determines that a guardian of my person should be appointed for me, then I nominate my primary agent as my guardian. If my primary agent is unable or unwilling to act as my guardian, then I nominate the alternate agent(s) whom I have named under Clause 1 above, in the order designated, as my guardian. No guardian appointed hereunder shall be required to post bond.

PART 2 - INSTRUCTIONS FOR HEALTHCARE

6. END-OF-LIFE DECISIONS

6.1 Except to the extent prohibited by law, I direct that my healthcare providers and others involved in my care provide, withhold, or withdraw treatment in accordance with the choices I have expressed below:

(initial only those options which apply)

Terminal Condition

_____ If, at any time, I have a medical condition certified to be a terminal condition by two physicians who have personally examined me, and the physicians have determined that my death could occur within a reasonably short period of time without the use of life-sustaining procedures then I direct that, save as may be set out herein, such life-sustaining procedures

(initial only the option immediately below which you want to apply)

_____ SHALL _____ SHALL NOT

be applied to prolong my life within the limits of generally accepted healthcare standards.

Specifically, and notwithstanding the foregoing, if I am suffering from a terminal condition I want to receive those treatments which I have initialed below and do not want to receive those which I have not initialed below:

(initial only the treatments below you want to receive)

______ artificial nutrition or hydration.

______ cardiac resuscitation or a cardiac pacemaker.

______ blood or blood products.

______ mechanical respiration.

______ kidney dialysis.

______ antibiotics.

______ any form of surgery or invasive diagnostic tests.

______ organs.

Permanent Unconsciousness

______ If, at any time, I have a medical condition certified to be terminal condition by two physicians who have personally examined me, and the physicians have certified that I am in a state of permanent unconsciousness and the application of life-sustaining procedures would serve only to prolong the dying process then I direct that, save as may be set out herein, such life-sustaining procedures

(initial only the option immediately below which you want to apply)

______ SHALL ______ SHALL NOT

be applied to prolong my life within the limits of generally accepted healthcare standards.

Specifically, and notwithstanding the foregoing, if I am in a persistent vegetative state or other condition of permanent unconsciousness I want to receive those treatments which I have initialed below and do not want to receive those which I have not initialed below:

(initial only the treatments below you want to receive)

______ artificial nutrition or hydration.

______ cardiac resuscitation or a cardiac pacemaker.

______ blood or blood products.

______ mechanical respiration.

______ kidney dialysis.

______ antibiotics.

______ any form of surgery or invasive diagnostic tests.

______ organs.

Maximum Treatment

______ I want to receive the maximum treatment in all possible circumstances to prolong my life.

7. RELIEF FROM PAIN

(initial one choice only)

______ I want to receive treatment for the alleviation of pain or discomfort.

______ I do not want to receive treatment for the alleviation of pain or discomfort.

8. PREGNANCY (Optional)

(If applicable, initial your choice below. If no choice is initialed, this clause shall cease to apply)

8.1 Should I become unconscious and I am pregnant, I direct that the end-of-life provisions in this document shall, unless applicable laws prescribe otherwise:

(initial one choice below)

______ continue to have full effect.

______ cease to have full effect.

PART 3 - ANATOMICAL GIFTS

9. ANATOMICAL GIFT AT DEATH (Optional)

(If applicable, initial your choice below. If no choice is initialed, this clause shall cease to apply)

9.1 Upon my death:

______ I do not wish to give any organs, tissues or other body parts and refuse to make an anatomical gift.

or

______ I hereby give any needed organs, tissues, or other body parts.

or

______ I give the following organs, tissues, or other body parts only:-

____

____

____

____.

9.2 If I have decided to donate organs under 9.1 above, then my gift shall be for the initialed purposes below only:

______ Transplant.

_____ Therapy.

_____ Research.

_____ Education.

PART 4 - PRIMARY PHYSICIAN

10. PRIMARY PHYSICIAN

10.1 I appoint ________________ of ______________________________ __ (Telephone:- ____________________) as my primary physician. If the aforementioned physician is unable or unwilling to act as my primary physician, then I appoint ________________ of __________________________ _____ (Telephone:- ____________________) as my alternate physician. If neither of the foregoing are willing and able to act as my primary physician, my primary physician shall be deemed to be the lead physician advising on my medical treatment.

PART 5 - GENERAL

11. EFFECT OF COPY

11.1 A copy of this form has the same effect as the original.

I sign my name to this Durable Power of Attorney for Healthcare & Living Will on this ____ day of ________, 20___ at ___________________________ in the State of_____________________________.

____

Signature of Principal

WITNESS AFFIDAVIT

I declare, on the basis of information and belief, that the person who signed or acknowledged this document (the "principal") is personally known to me (or has proven their identity to me), that he/she signed or acknowledged this Durable Power of Attorney for Healthcare & Living Will in my presence, and that he/she appears to be of sound mind and under no duress, fraud, or undue influence. I am not related to the principal by blood, marriage, or adoption, either as a spouse, a lineal ancestor, descendant of the parents of the principal, or spouse of any of them. I am not directly financially responsible for the principal's medical care. I am not entitled to any portion of the principal's estate upon his/her decease, whether under any will or as an heir by intestate succession, nor am I the beneficiary of an insurance policy on the principal's life, nor do I have a claim against the principal's estate as of this time. I am not the principal's attending physician, nor an employee of the attending physician. No more than one witness is an employee of a health facility in which the principal is a patient. I am not appointed as a healthcare agent or successor healthcare agent by this document.

Witness No. 1

Signature: ______________________________

Print Name: ______________________________

Residence Address: ______________________________

____

____

____

Telephone: ______________________________

Date: ______________________________

Witness No. 2

Signature: ______________________________

Print Name: ______________________________

Residence Address: ______________________________

____

____

____

Telephone: ______________________________

Date: ______________________________

NOTARY AFFIDAVIT

STATE OF ______________ **COUNTY OF ______________**

On ________________ before me, _______________________, a notary public, personally appeared _______________________________, who proved to me on the basis of satisfactory evidence to be the person whose name is subscribed to the within instrument and acknowledged to me that he/she executed the same in his/her authorized capacity, and that by his/her signature on the instrument he/she executed the instrument. I certify under PENALTY OF PERJURY that the foregoing is true and correct. Witness my hand and official seal.

Signature: ___________________________________

Print Name: __________________________________

My commission expires on: ____________________

(Seal)

APPENDIX 3

NOTICE OF REVOCATION

Downloadable Forms

Blank copies of this form are available to download from our website.

Web: http://www.enodare.com/downloadarea/

Unlock Code: YUK20150

enodare

DATED THIS ____ DAY OF _____________, 20___.

____

NOTICE OF REVOCATION

of

____

(Principal)

____

www.enodare.com

NOTICE OF REVOCATION

I, ______________________________ of ____________________________________

____

_______ aged eighteen years and upwards hereby revoke, countermand and make null and void the Durable Power of Attorney for Healthcare & Living Will dated __________________ (the "Power of Attorney") and granted in favor of ________ ______________________________ (the "Agent", which expression shall include any successor agent appointed under the Power of Attorney) and all rights, powers and authority thereby given to the Agent shall hereby lapse and cease.

Executed this ______________ day of ____________________________________, 20 ________, at ____.

____

THE PRINCIPAL

WITNESS AFFIDAVIT

I declare, on the basis of information and belief, that the person who signed or acknowledged this document (the "principal") is personally known to me, that he/she signed or acknowledged this Notice of Revocation of a Power of Attorney in my presence, and that he/she appears to be of sound mind and under no duress, fraud, or undue influence. I am not related to the principal by blood, marriage, or adoption, either as a spouse, a lineal ancestor, descendant of the parents of the principal, or spouse of any of them. I am not directly financially responsible for the principal's medical care. I am not entitled to any portion of the principal's estate upon his/her decease, whether under any Will or as an heir by intestate succession, nor am I the beneficiary of an insurance policy on the principal's life, nor do I have a claim against the principal's estate as of this time. I am not the principal's attending physician, nor an employee of the attending physician. No more than one witness is an employee of a health facility in which the principal is a patient. I am not appointed as healthcare agent or successor healthcare agent by this document.

Witness No. 1

Signature: ________________________________

Date: ________________________________

Print Name: ________________________________

Telephone: ________________________________

Residence Address: ________________________________

Witness No. 2

Signature: ________________________________

Date: ________________________________

Print Name: ________________________________

Telephone: ________________________________

Residence Address: ________________________________

NOTARY AFFIDAVIT

STATE OF ______________ **COUNTY OF** ______________

On ________________ before me, ________________________, a notary public, personally appeared _____________________________, who proved to me on the basis of satisfactory evidence to be the person whose name is subscribed to the within instrument and acknowledged to me that he/she executed the same in his/her authorized capacity, and that by his/her signature on the instrument he/she executed the instrument. I certify under PENALTY OF PERJURY that the foregoing is true and correct. Witness my hand and official seal.

Signature: ___________________________________

Print Name: _________________________________

My commission expires on: _____________________

(Seal)

Other Great Books from Enodare's Estate Planning Series

Make Your Own Last Will & Testament

By making a will, you can provide for the distribution of your assets to your love ones, appoint guardians to care for your children, provide for the management of gifts to young adults and children, specify how your debts are to be paid following your death, make funeral arrangements and much more.

This book will guide you through the entire process of making a will. It contains all the forms that you will need to make a valid legal will, simply and easily.

2nd Edition
enodare
Make Your Own
Living Trust
& Avoid Probate
- Avoid the delays and costs of probate
- Manage your assets during incapacity
- Leave money and property to your loved ones
- Save money and reduce taxes

Living Trust Forms Included!
Estate Planning Series

Make Your Own Living Trust & Avoid Probate

Living trusts are used to distribute a person's assets after they die in a manner that avoids the costs, delays and publicity of probate. They also cater for the management of property during periods of incapacity.

This book will guide you step-by-step through the process of creating your very own living trust, transferring assets to your living trust and subsequently managing those assets.

All relevant forms are included.

Make Your Own Living Will

Do you want a say in what life sustaining medical treatments you receive during periods in which you are incapacitated and either in a permanent state of unconsciousness or suffering from a terminal illness? Well if so, you must have a living will!

This book will introduce you to living wills, the types of medical procedures that they cover, the matters that you need to consider when making them and, of course, provide you with all the relevant forms you need to make your own living will!

www.enodare.com

Other Great Books from Enodare's Estate Planning Series

enodare
Estate Planning Essentials
3rd Edition
Learn How To:
- Prepare an effective estate plan
- Provide for children and other beneficiaries
- Plan for medical incapacity
- Save on legal fees & taxes
- & much more......

Estate Planning Worksheets Included!
Estate Planning Series

Estate Planning Essentials

This book is a must read for anyone who doesn't already have a comprehensive estate plan.

It will show you the importance of having wills, trusts, powers of attorney and living wills in your estate plan. You will learn about the probate process, why people are so keen to avoid it and lots of simple methods you can actually use to do so. You will learn about reducing estate taxes and how best to provide for young beneficiaries and children.

This book is a great way to get you started on the way to making your own estate plan.

How to Probate an Estate - A Step-By-Step Guide for Executors

This book is essential reading for anyone contemplating acting as an executor of someone's estate!

Learn about the various stages of probate and what an executor needs to do at each stage to successfully navigate his way through to closing the estate and distributing the deceased's assets.

You will learn how an executor initiates probate, locates and manages assets, deals with debt and taxes, distributes assets, and much more. This is a fantastic step-by-step guide through the entire process!

Funeral Planning Basics - A Step-By-Step Guide to Funeral Planning

Through proper funeral planning, you can ensure that your loved ones are not confronted with the unnecessary burden of having to plan a funeral at a time which is already very traumatic for them.

This book will introduce you to issues such as organ donations, purchasing caskets, cremation, burial, purchasing grave plots, organization of funeral services, legal and financial issues, costs of pre-arranging a funeral, how to save money on funerals, how to finance funerals and much more.

www.enodare.com

Healthcare Power of Attorney

Appoint someone you trust to make medical decisions for you if you become mentally incapacitated.

Power of Attorney for Finance and Property

Appoint someone you trust to manage your financial affairs if you become mentally incapacitated, or if you are unable to do so for any reason.

And More.........

Enodare's Will Writer software also includes documents such as self proving Affidavits, Deeds of Assignment, Certifications of Trust, Estate Planning Worksheet, Revocation forms and more.

The documents are valid in all states except Louisiana.

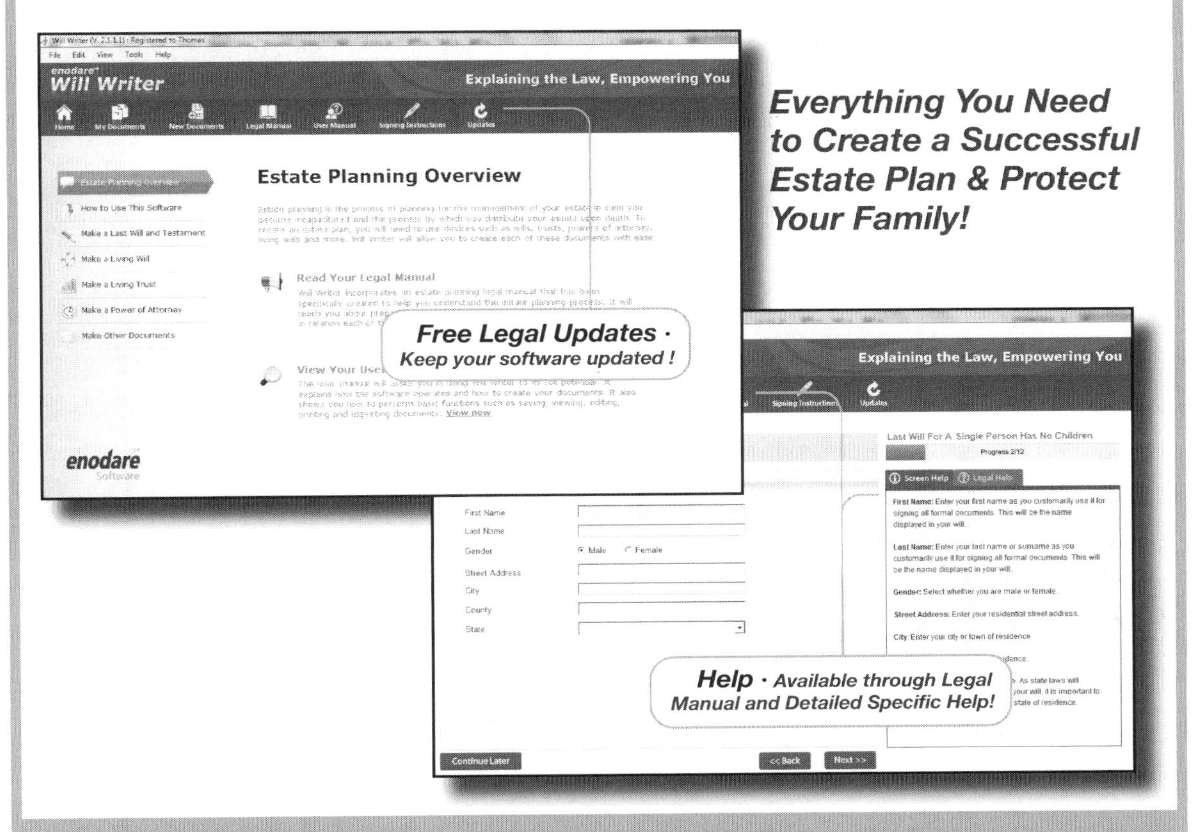

Ensure
Your Family's
Protected

Entrepreneur's Guide to Starting a Business

Entrepreneur's Guide to Starting a Business takes the fear of the unknown out of starting your new business and provides a treasure chest of information that will help you be successful from the very start.

First-time entrepreneurs face a daunting challenge in identifying all of the issues that must be addressed and mastered when starting a new business. If any item slips through the cracks, or is handled improperly, it could bring a new company crashing to the ground. Entrepreneur's Guide to Starting a Business helps you meet that challenge by walking you through all of the important aspects of successfully launching your own business.

When you finish reading this book, not alone will you know the step-by-step process needed to turn your business idea and vision into a successful reality, but you'll also have a wealth of practical knowledge about corporate structures, business & marketing plans, e-commerce, hiring staff & external advisors, finding commercial property, sales & marketing, legal & financial matters, tax and much more.

- Comprehensive overview of all major aspects of starting a new business
- Covers every stage of the process, from writing your business plan to marketing and selling your new product
- Plain English descriptions of complex subject matters
- Real-world case study showing you how things play out in an actual new business environment

NEW TITLE

Personal Budget Kit

Budgeting Made Easy

In this kit, we'll guide you step-by-step through the process of creating and living with a personal budget. We'll show you how analyze how you receive and spend your money and to set goals, both short and long-term.

You'll learn how to gain control of your personal cash flow. You'll discover when you need to make adjustments to your budget and how to do it wisely. Most of all, this kit will show you that budgeting isn't simply about adding limitations to your living but rather the foundation for living better by maximizing the resources you have.

This Personal Budget Kit provides you with step-by-step instructions, detailed information and all the budget worksheets and spreadsheets necessary to identify and understand your spending habits, reduce your expenses, set goals, prepare personal budgets, monitor your progress and take control over your finances.

- Reduce your spending painlessly and effortlessly
- Pay off your debts early
- Improve your credit rating
- Save & invest money
- Set & achieve financial goals
- Eliminate financial worries

enodare **NEW TITLE**